TORRANCE PUBLIC LIBRARY

3 2111 01490 1554

P9-CDT-203

**Katy Geissert
Civic Center Library**
3301 Torrance Blvd.
Torrance, CA 90503

MALALA

A BRAVE GIRL FROM PAKISTAN

by JEANETTE WINTER

BEACH LANE BOOKS

New York London Toronto Sydney New Delhi

The story of Iqbal Masih has stayed with me since I read his obituary on April 19, 1995, three days after he was shot. I learned about his life and about the courage he showed speaking out against bonded slavery for children in the carpet trade in Pakistan.

When I read on October 9, 2012, of Malala Yousafzai being shot for speaking out for the right of girls to attend school in Pakistan, I thought again of Iqbal.

Two courageous children whose bravery transcended their youth came together in my mind—and led to this book.

—J. W.

BEACH LANE BOOKS
An imprint of Simon & Schuster Children's Publishing Division
1230 Avenue of the Americas, New York, New York 10020
Copyright © 2014 by Jeanette Winter
"Iqbal" author's note originally published in a slightly different form in *Tikvah: Children's Book Creators Reflect on Human Rights* (New York: SeaStar Books, 1999), 84. Used by permission from Chronicle Books, San Francisco. Visit www.ChronicleBooks.com.
All rights reserved, including the right of reproduction in whole or in part in any form.
BEACH LANE BOOKS is a trademark of Simon & Schuster, Inc.
For information about special discounts for bulk purchases, please contact Simon & Schuster Special Sales at 1-866-506-1949 or business@simonandschuster.com.
The Simon & Schuster Speakers Bureau can bring authors to your live event. For more information or to book an event, contact the Simon & Schuster Speakers Bureau at 1-866-248-3049 or visit our website at www.simonspeakers.com.
Book design by Ann Bobco and Vikki Sheatsley
The text for this book is set in ITC Newtext BT.
Manufactured in China
0814 SCP
First Edition
10 9 8 7 6 5 4 3 2 1
CIP data for this book is available from the Library of Congress.
ISBN 978-1-4814-2294-9
ISBN 978-1-4814-2295-6 (eBook)

AUTHOR'S NOTE

Two children from Pakistan spoke out against injustice in their world. Their bravery in the face of great danger is an inspiration to all who know their stories.

MALALA YOUSAFZAI
1997–

Malala was born in the small town of Mingora, in the Swat Valley of Pakistan. She lived with her mother, father, and two brothers. Malala started school early at the school her father ran, and excelled in her studies.

The Taliban, a group of religious extremists, had gained power in the Swat Valley and discouraged girls from attending school. Malala asked her father, "Why don't they want girls to go to school?" "They are scared of the pen," he replied.

When Malala was only eleven, she first spoke publicly about the importance of education for girls. Even as the Taliban became more aggressive, Malala continued to speak out. The threats continued, never stopping Malala—until the day a Taliban fighter shot her as she rode home in a school van. The bullet went through her head and neck to her shoulder. Malala was treated in many hospitals, and finally in the Queen Elizabeth Hospital Birmingham in England, where she now lives with her family.

Malala has received many awards for bravery, including the International Children's Peace Prize (runner-up), the Pakistan National Youth Peace Prize, the Mother Teresa Memorial International Award for Social Justice, and the Rome Prize for Peace and Humanitarian Action. In 2013, she was a Nobel Peace Prize nominee.

She continues to recover and she continues to speak out.

Let us not pray to be sheltered
from dangers,
but to be fearless when
facing them.

RABINDRANATH TAGORE

"Who is Malala?" the Taliban fighter demands, looking into the school van.

Malala is a girl who isn't afraid.

"I will power myself with knowledge," she says.

"Don't go to school,"
  the Taliban fighters tell the girls in Swat Valley.
"Don't read," they say.
  The girls don't listen.
  They are brave girls.

The schoolroom holds their sun
and blocks the threatening shadows.
But away from school, a dark cloud
follows them everywhere.

Every day the Taliban broadcast their warnings.

"No school for girls," they say.

But Malala is a brave girl who speaks out.

"I have the right of education.
I have the right to play.
I have the right to sing.
I have the right to talk.
I have the right to go to market.
I have the right to SPEAK UP."

The brave girls of Swat Valley outwit the Taliban fighters by wearing everyday clothes to school. Their uniforms stay hidden at home.

Malala speaks out again and again.

"They cannot stop me.
I will get my education,
if it is home, school, or anyplace."

There is no peace in Swat Valley.

The Taliban burn and bomb the schools.

Still Malala speaks out.

"The extremists are afraid of books and pens.
They are afraid of women.
How dare the Taliban take away
my basic right to education?"

Attending school becomes more and more dangerous.

Girls travel to and from school in a van, for safety.

Until one day, a Taliban fighter stops the van,

looks inside, and demands,

"Who is Malala?

Speak up, otherwise I will shoot you all."

He shoots Malala.

The van rushes her to the small hospital in Swat Valley.

A helicopter lifts her to a bigger hospital far away.

A jet plane flies her across the ocean to a still bigger hospital.

Everywhere, the doctors work to save her.

The shot fired at Malala is heard the world over.
Prayers from girls and boys, women and men
surround her bedside.
Slowly, Malala wakes from the nightmare.
She opens her eyes, holds a book, and smiles.
And her voice returns.

On Malala's 16th birthday, before world leaders,
she speaks out again, stronger than before.

"They thought that bullets would silence us,
but they failed. . . .
One child, one teacher,
one book, one pen,
can change the world."

The world hears the voice of this brave girl from
Pakistan and listens.

At his funeral,
800 mourners wept
for this brave boy
from Pakistan.

Back home, the threats continue.
They still don't scare this twelve-year-old boy.
Iqbal lives free.
Until the day a bullet takes his life
as he rides his bicycle.

Iqbal goes to carpet factories all over Pakistan.
He spreads the message of freedom
to over 3,000 bonded children.
And he travels across the ocean to speak out
in America.

"I would like to do what Abraham Lincoln did.
I would like to do it in Pakistan.
I would like to free children in bondage."

A liberated boy, Iqbal starts school.

A smart boy, he flies through his studies.

A brave boy, he speaks out for children like him.

Threats from factory owners don't scare

this ten-year-old boy.

He runs to the dark factory,
waving the notice, shouting,
"You are free! We are free!"

Iqbal steps inside,
and learns that *Peshgi* has been outlawed—
all loans are forgiven.
The carpet boss doesn't own him anymore.
Iqbal is free.

Trudging home one night,
Iqbal sees a notice on a wall—
announcing a meeting about *Peshgi*,
the loans that hold children like Iqbal in bondage.

Iqbal lives in darkness.

He walks to the factory before the sun comes up,

works all day in the gloom,

and heads home after the sun sets.

Tiny fingers can make intricate patterns,
so complex that the boss doesn't see
Iqbal weaving his kite into a carpet section.
His hands work, while his mind soars.

Iqbal sees rows of children chained like him,
weaving carpets in the sweltering dimness.

Iqbal is chained to the loom,
lest he try to escape.

"No kites here!" the carpet boss bellows,
as he pulls Iqbal into the dark factory.
The only window has bars on it.

TWELVE DOLLARS!

Until the twelve-dollar loan to his parents is repaid, four-year-old Iqbal must work in the carpet factory. Twelve dollars for a boy's freedom.

Let us not pray to be sheltered
from dangers,
but to be fearless when
facing them.

RABINDRANATH TAGORE

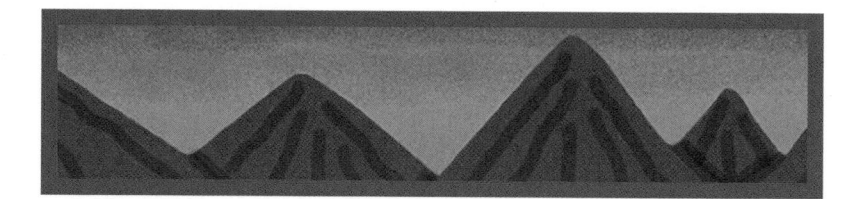

AUTHOR'S NOTE

Two children from Pakistan spoke out against injustice in their world. Their bravery in the face of great danger is an inspiration to all who know their stories.

IQBAL MASIH
1982–1995

Iqbal Masih was born in the village of Muridke, near Lahore, in Pakistan. When he was only four years old, his extremely poor parents borrowed twelve dollars from the owner of a carpet factory. In return for the loan, Iqbal became a bonded worker, shackled every day to a carpet loom until the loan was repaid. He earned twenty cents a day.

At ten, Iqbal was liberated by the Bonded Liberation Front of Pakistan. After he gained his freedom, Iqbal bravely spoke out against child labor.

Iqbal's accounts of the horrors of his experiences spread. He traveled far from home to tell his story.

Iqbal spoke at an international labor conference in Stockholm. In Boston he received an award from the Reebok Human Rights Foundation. The United Nations High Commissioner for Human Rights honored Iqbal as a "champion of the fight in Pakistan against contemporary forms of slavery which affects millions of children worldwide."

Iqbal wanted to study law. Brandeis University offered him a full scholarship as soon as he was ready.

At home, Iqbal received death threats from people in the carpet industry. As he and two cousins rode bicycles in their village on April 16, 1995, Iqbal was shot and killed. He was twelve years old. The circumstances of his death are murky.

The story of Iqbal Masih has stayed with me since I read his obituary on April 19, 1995, three days after he was shot. I learned about his life and about the courage he showed speaking out against bonded slavery for children in the carpet trade in Pakistan.

When I read on October 9, 2012, of Malala Yousafzai being shot for speaking out for the right of girls to attend school in Pakistan, I thought again of Iqbal.

Two courageous children whose bravery transcended their youth came together in my mind—and led to this book.

—J. W.

IQBAL

A BRAVE BOY FROM PAKISTAN

by JEANETTE WINTER

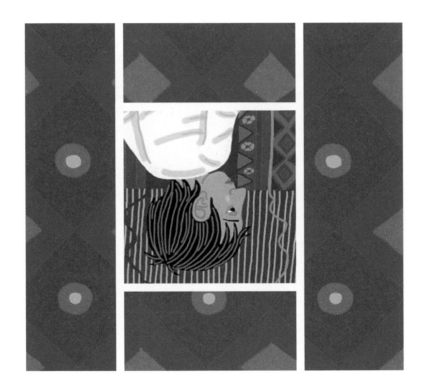

BEACH LANE BOOKS

New York London Toronto Sydney New Delhi